Santa's Sackful OF BEST Christmas Ideas

DERI ROBINS

ILLUSTRATED BY GEORGE BUCHANAN

Kingfisher Books

Kingfisher Books, Grisewood & Dempsey Ltd, Elsley House,
24-30 Great Titchfield Street, London W1P 7AD

First published in 1993 by Kingfisher Books
2 4 6 8 10 9 7 5 3 1
Copyright © Grisewood & Dempsey Ltd 1993

BRITISH LIBRARY CATALOGUING IN PUBLICATION DATA
A catalogue record for this book is available from
the British Library

ISBN 1 85697 109 0

Typeset in 3B2 by Tracey McNerney
Phototypeset by Southern Positives and Negatives (SPAN)
Printed in Spain

Designed by Brian Robertson and George Buchanan
Cover design by Terry Woodley

Contents

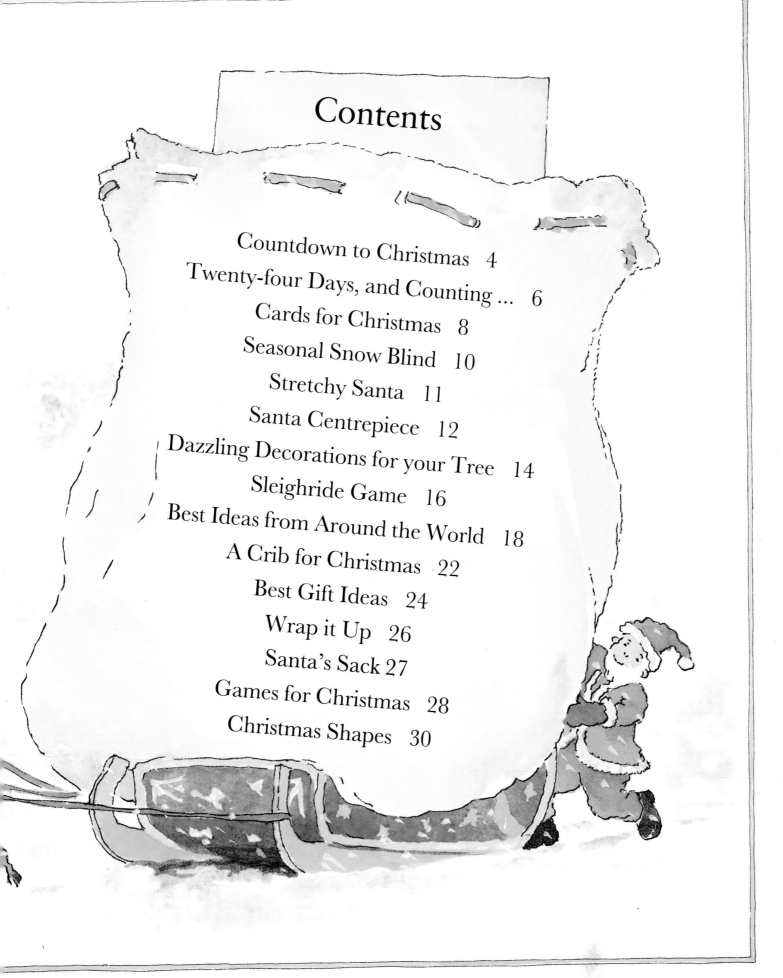

Countdown to Christmas

November 30

Hang up your new advent calendar.

December 1

Write out your Christmas card list.

December 2

Print home-made cards (pages 8-9)...

December 7

Make a crib scene (pages 22-23).

December 8

Print some wrapping paper (page 26).

December 9

Make paper chains – cut strips from magazines, and link together with glue.

December 14

Collect pine cones to decorate.

December 15

Learn the verses of a carol.

December 16

Make a pinata (page 20).

December 17

Try out your carol on a favourite neighbour.

December 21

Deck the halls with holly!

December 22

Do some cooking (pages 18-21).

December 23

Wrap up the presents.

December 3

...and post them!

December 4

Make a stained glass window from card and tissue paper.

December 5

Make presents (pages 24-25)...

December 6

...and post your own present list to Santa!

December 10

Start making some new decorations...

December 11

...make dough shapes for the tree (page 14)...

December 12

...a Santa wobbler (page 11)..

December 13

...or a little centrepiece for the Christmas table.

December 18

No snow? Make a snow blind! (page 10.)

December 19

Put out treats for the birds (page 19).

December 20

Hang up your cards on lengths of ribbon, or make a coat-hanger mobile.

December 24

Don't forget the mince pies and sherry!

The Night Before Christmas!

Twenty-four Days, and Counting...

The four weeks leading up to Christmas are known as Advent. This used to be a time of fasting – now it's more likely to be full of fun and busy preparation. This Advent calendar takes a little bit of time and patience to make, but it's well worth the effort – it can be packed away after Christmas, and used for many years to come.

You will need:
24 empty matchboxes
24 tiny paperclips
24 split pins
stiff card
sellotape
poster paints
PVA glue
24 tiny gifts
or decorations

1 Take the drawers out of the match-boxes. Glue the boxes into a tower.

2 Push a split pin through one end of each drawer, and slot them into the tower.

3 Number each drawer from 1 – 24.

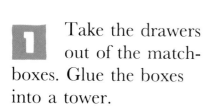
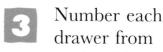

6

4 Trace the large tree from page 30 onto card, and paint one side green. Bend the clips into hooks, and stick them through the tree.

front of tree

Use a piece of tape to stick each paperclip to the back of the tree. Glue the tree to one side of the matchboxes.

back of tree

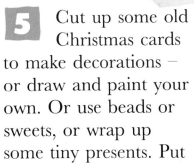

5 Cut up some old Christmas cards to make decorations – or draw and paint your own. Or use beads or sweets, or wrap up some tiny presents. Put a gift or decoration in each drawer. On each day in Advent, take a decoration from the right drawer, and hang it on the tree.

Cards for Christmas

In 1864, the world's first Christmas cards went on sale. The idea proved to be amazingly popular, and by 1900 people were already being advised to post early for Christmas!

*You will need:
Some thin card; scissors; glue; tracing paper; scraps of paper or fabric; paints.*

STAND-UP CARDS

1 Trace a red template from pages 31-32 onto card. Do this twice.

2 Cut out the two shapes, and paint both sides.

3 Cut a slit from the top of one shape to the middle. On the other shape, cut from the bottom to the middle.

Slot together and fold flat to send!

design your own cards!

WINDOW SCENE

1 Fold a piece of card in half. Draw a big window on the front, and cut out.

2 Glue on scraps of fabric or paper for the walls, curtains and tree. Glue sequins or paper stars to the tree.

3 Use a pencil to sketch the view through the window. Then open the card, and paint the scene in full.

CHRISTMAS CRACKERS

1 Cut a strip of card, about 60 x 6 cm. Divide into six equal parts.

2 Fold up as shown. Draw a cracker on the front, and cut out.

3 Paint and decorate. Glue on glitter, shiny stars or sequins.

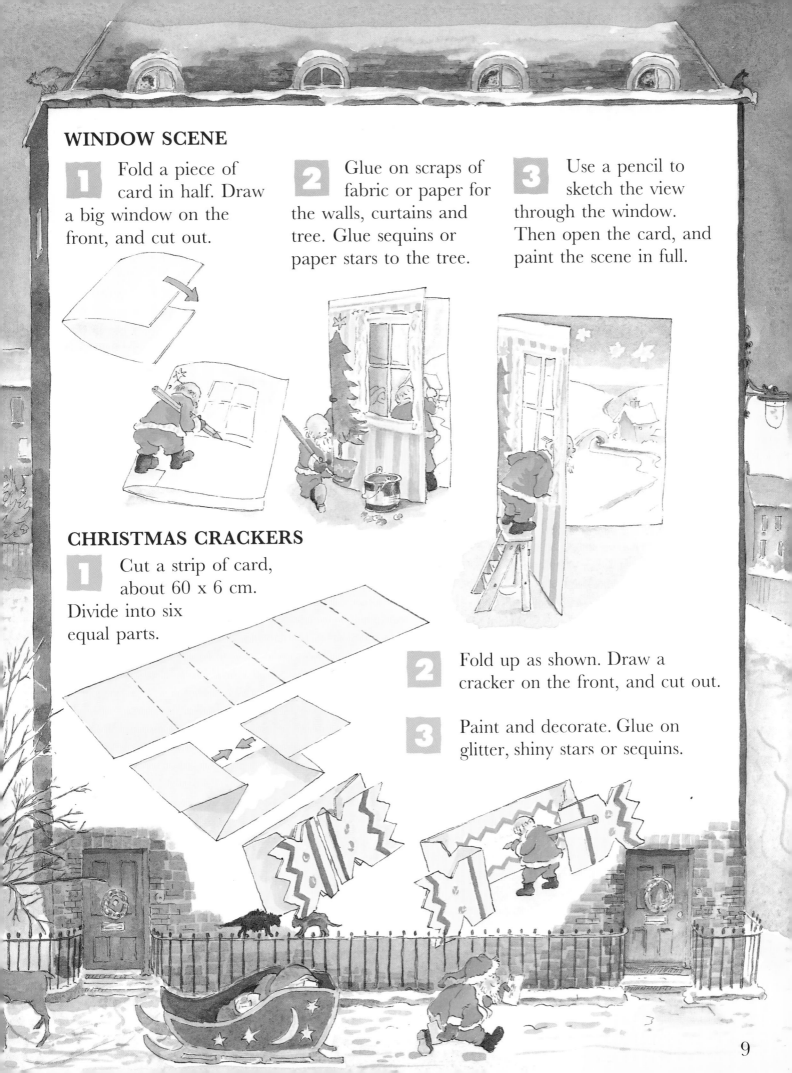

Seasonal Snow Blind

Snow, snow and more snow – that's the forecast for the North Pole this Christmas. If there's none coming your way, try making this snowy scene to hang up in the window.

1 Tape several sheets of sugar paper together, and cut into a big window frame.

4 Cut stars and a moon from silver foil, and glue to the scene. Draw and cut the other features from card, and glue these on too.

You will need: Black sugar paper; blue tissue paper; scissors; glue; paints; silver foil; card.

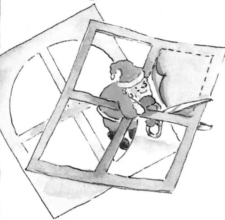

2 Cut the window panes from tissue paper. Make them slightly larger than the holes in the frame. Glue them to the frame.

3 Paint a snowy scene onto the tissue paper.

Stretchy Santa

Here's a Santa wobbler to hang from the ceiling.

1 Take a large, thin strip of card or paper (wallpaper offcuts are good). Paint it bright red, and paint a belt about 3/4 of the way

You will need:
Thin card or wallpaper;
paints; cotton wool;
glue; thread; plasticene.

down. Paint on the fur trim. When the paint has dried, fold the paper in half and make cuts with the scissors as shown here.

2 Cut the head, hands and feet from card. Paint and glue to the body. Glue on a cotton wool beard.

3 Hang the wobbler up with thread or ribbon. To make the body stretch, stick plasticene or some small weight behind the feet.

try making some more stretchy figures

Santa Centrepiece

As the figures in this card model slot together, they can easily be taken apart and stored when Christmas is over.

You will need:
Thin white card
Tracing paper
Glue
Cotton
Paints
Cotton wool

1 Trace all the blue templates on page 32. Rub down onto the card, and cut them out carefully.

glue

glue

fold

fold

fold

glue

glue top
to base

2 Fold up the tabs of the sleigh, and glue them into place. Stick to the base of the sleigh. When the glue has dried, paint the sleigh with silver or gold paint.

3 Paint one side of the Santa's body, arms and feet. Glue on a cotton wool beard.

4 Curl up the body and glue down the back tab. Glue the arms around the body, and glue the feet inside the front of the Santa.

slot body
onto legs

7 Paint the little gift boxes before you glue them together. Fold inwards along all the lines, and glue the side flaps only. Leave the top flap open.

top flap

5 Trace off and cut out at least six reindeer, so that you have a whole herd trekking across the tablecloth! Paint both sides of each reindeer part.

6 Cut slots, and push the legs into the body as shown above. Don't make the slots too wide, or the legs will fall out of the body.

8 Make a box for everyone at the table. Put a tiny present (or a message) into each box, and fold down the top flap.

9 Pile up the presents in the sleigh. Stand the Santa figure in front, and link him to his team of reindeers with reins made from cotton.

Dazzling Decorations for Your Tree

The elves made a wonderful job of decorating the tree this year. Here are some of their best ideas...

DOUGH SHAPES

You will need: 150 g plain flour; 1 tbsp salt; 5 tbsp cold water; half a tbsp cooking oil; pastry cutters; a knitting needle; paints; a grown-up helper.

1 Mix the flour, salt, oil and water. Knead until smooth and stretchy.

2 Roll out on a floured surface, until the dough is about 6 mm thick.

3 Cut shapes from the dough – use the cutters, or carefully cut out with a knife. Make a hole at the top of each shape with a knitting needle.

4 Ask your grown-up helper to bake the shapes in a oven (130°C/250°F/gas mark ¹/₂), for about 40 minutes.

5 Paint the shapes when cool. Add glue and glitter, and a final coat of clear varnish if you like.

6 Thread ribbon through the holes.

CONE FIGURES

Small pine cones can be painted and dipped in glitter – or turned into little people and animals by sticking on card and other bits and pieces.

card beak

This robin has a card beak, a feather tail, and card eyes.

This tree has a base made from the top of a toothpaste tube.

Make a reindeer with card ears, eyes, antlers and a painted nose.

toothpaste-tube tops

doily wings

A white-painted cone with a toothpaste-tube hat and paper scarf makes a snowman!

Narrow cones make good angels – use a cork or a cotton pulp ball (from a craft shop) for the head.

Sleighride Game

All you need to play this game is a dice and a button or counter for each player. Put all the counters on the START square, and take it in turns to throw the dice. Move your counters around the board, following the direction shown by the numbers.

If you land on the bottom of one of the sleighs, slide UP to the yellow star. If you land on the top of one of the chimneys, slide DOWN to the yellow parcel. The first player to land on the FINISH square with an exact throw of the dice wins the game.

Best Ideas from Around the World

The spirit of Christmas is the same wherever you go – but different countries have their own ways of celebrating the great event...

SWEDISH GINGERSNAPS

You will need:
230 g butter
230 g brown sugar
2 egg whites
400 g plain flour
1 tsp bicarbonate of
soda
1 tsp ground ginger
1 tsp ground cloves
1 tsp ground
cinnamon

1 Mix the sugar and butter until light and fluffy. Beat in the egg whites.

2 Sieve in the flour, spices and soda. Mix well, to form a dough.

DANISH HEARTS

You will need:
2 different-coloured pieces of paper, folded in half; scissors; ribbon.

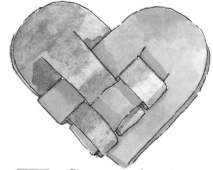

folded →
← edge

1 Trace the orange shape from page 31 onto both pieces of paper.

2 Cut out the two shapes, and cut up the middle lines.

3 Roll out the dough until 6 mm thick.

5 Bake for 10-12 minutes at 170°C/350°F/gas mark 4.

4 Cut into Christmas shapes. Make holes at the top of each shape.

6 Decorate with icing sugar mixed with water and food colouring.

Hang on the tree with ribbon.

fircones spread with unsalted peanut butter

unsalted nuts

apples studded with mixed seeds

sweetcorn

3 Weave the hearts together, as shown in the four pictures. Make holes in the top, thread with ribbon and hang up.

FINNISH BIRD TREATS

In Finland, many country people refuse to sit down to Christmas dinner until the birds have been fed. Try putting out these treats (and some fresh water) for the birds in your garden this Christmas.

19

MEXICAN PIÑATA

In Mexican homes at Christmas, pots called piñatas are hung from the ceiling. Children hit the pots with sticks until they burst, showering them with sweets, toys – sometimes even water!

1 Mix up the paste, and tear the paper into strips. Dip the strips into the paste. Cover the balloon with six layers of paper, and leave to dry.

2 Try turning the piñata into an animal, by gluing on features made from cardboard.

3 Cut the top off the piñata, and pull out the balloon.

4 Paint with poster paints. Seal with a coat of varnish. Make two holes in the top, and thread with ribbon. Fill the piñata, and tape the top back.

You will need:
Newspaper; wallpaper paste; a blown-up balloon; sticky tape; paints; varnish

AUSTRALIAN CHRISTMAS PUDDING

You will need:
A large container of vanilla ice-cream; 1 tsp cinnamon; 1 tbsp of: raisins, sultanas, glacé cherries, dried apricots, prunes, pineapple, crystallized ginger, lemon or orange peel and unsalted mixed nuts.

FRENCH LOG

In parts of France, a rich, log-shaped cake is eaten on Christmas Eve. Yule logs are special in many countries at Christmas. They stand for warmth and light during the winter, and are thought to bring luck in the coming year.

You will need:
1 packet ginger biscuits
1 tsp cocoa
1 tsp icing sugar
1 cup double cream

1 Whisk cream, cocoa and sugar together until stiff.

2 Use half the cream to sandwich all but one of the biscuits together.

3 Cover with rest of cream. Break the last biscuit into a twig.

4 Chill until needed, and sprinkle with extra icing sugar.

1 Empty the ice-cream into a bowl. Leave until slightly soft.

2 Chop up the fruit and nuts, and mix into the ice-cream. Stir in the cinnamon.

3 Put into a plastic pudding basin.

4 Cover with foil, and freeze for two hours or until needed.

Loosen the sides, and turn out onto a plate.

A Crib for Christmas

Did you know that the very first Christmas crib was life-sized, with real people and animals

standing in for the figures in the Christmas story? It was set up by St Francis of Assisi, in his tiny chapel in Italy over 700 years ago. The crib was copied all over Europe, and many homes now have their own model version.

THE FIGURES

You will need: 9 strips of thin card; glue; paperclips; paper; paint; fabric scraps.

1 Copy this shape onto the strips, and cut away the shaded area.

10cm

7cm

cut away shaded area

2 Paint each of the figures – you'll need to make Mary, Joseph, three shepherds, three kings and an angel. Curl the shapes into cylinders, and glue in

THE STABLE

You will need: a shoebox; scissors; some small twigs or sticks; straw; a piece of blue tissue paper; paints and glue.

1 Cut a window in the back of the box, and paint the inside brown.

2 Glue tissue paper to the window, and paint on a star.

3 Glue twigs to the outside of the box. Glue five small twigs together to make a little manger. Put straw in the manger, and over the floor.

place – use paperclips to hold them in position while the glue sets.

3 Cut strips for arms – each 8 x 1 cm. Cut hands at each end, and paint one side. Glue around the bodies.

4 Add paper wings, golden haloes and

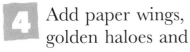

glue the arms around the bodies

crowns to the figures. You could also glue on wool or cotton wool for hair and beards, or scraps of fabric for clothes. A shepherd could also have a crook made from a pipe cleaner.

5 Make a baby Jesus from a smaller strip.

THE ANIMALS

Fold a piece of card in half, and draw the animals with their backs along the folds. Make the ass and the ox about 5 cm high, and the sheep 3 cm.

Paint and cut out the animals. Glue cotton wool over the sheep's body.

Best Gift Ideas

NOTEBOOKS

You will need:
Thin card; sheets of paper;
scissors; paints; a needle
and thread.

1 Lay five sheets of paper on top of the card. Trim all the sheets to the same size with scissors.

2 Fold the card and paper in half, as shown.

3 Draw a shape onto the front, and cut out with scissors – but leave most of the folded edge uncut.

4 Sew down the middle with a needle and thread. Follow the diagram on the right.

5 Paint the front of the notebook.

SPECIAL BOXES

You will need:
A box with a lid; paints;
glue; old magazines or
wrapping paper; varnish.

1 Paint the box. Leave to dry.

2 Cut pictures from the magazines or wrapping paper. Glue them over the box.

3 Coat each side with varnish.

PAPERWEIGHT

You will need:
Some red fabric; felt scraps;
two buttons; glue; scissors;
needle and thread; pins;
dried peas.

1 Trace the purple template from page 31. Cut out, to make a paper pattern.

2 Fold the fabric in half, and pin the pattern on top.

3 Sew all around the pattern, leaving a gap at the bottom.

4 Cut out, allowing 1 cm extra all round. Turn inside out, and glue on a felt beard and trimmings. Sew on buttons for eyes.

5 Fill with dried peas or beans. Sew up the hole.

Wrap It Up

As well as the printers shown below, you will need some thick paint and some large sheets of plain paper.

POTATO PRINTS

Cut a large potato in half with a knife.

Press a pastry cutter into one of the cut sides, and trim with the knife.

Cover the shape with thick paint.

Press down to print!

SNOWFLAKES

Brush paint over a paper doily to print a snowflake!

LEAF PRINTS

Paint the underside of a leaf. Press down to print.

STRING PRINTS

Cover a block of wood with glue.

Arrange a piece of string in a pattern on top (back to front!). Brush with paint and print.

Santa's Sack

If your present is an awkward shape, pop it into this special sack! All you need is some card, paints and glue.

glue flaps

fold

B

cut cut cut

B

B A B A B

1 Draw and paint this pattern onto card. It can be any size, but make all the *A*s the same and all the *B*s the same.

2 Cut the flaps, and fold up as shown. Glue the bottom and side flaps together.

3 Fold another piece of card in half. Draw a Santa face onto the front.

cut paper arms and feet, and glue these on too!

feet

arms

4 Cut out to make two separate heads. Cut handles out.

5 Paint the heads, and glue to the sack as shown above.

27

Games for Christmas

If you're fed up with all the usual games, try some of the North Pole favourites shown below!

CHRISTMAS CARD BINGO

You will need to draw a bingo card for each member of the family – each card should show the same 20 pictures, but in a different order.

DRAW A CAROL

The players divide into two teams. One player from each team thinks of a carol. They must then try to draw that carol, while the other members of their team guess what it is. The team that guesses their carol first wins that round. Keep going until you run out of carols! (When you do, try guessing the title of films, books, TV shows, etc.)

When the post arrives each day in December, check the Christmas cards. If one shows a star, for example, cross a star off your card. The winner is the first to cross out a whole horizontal row.

'Good King Wenceslas'

MELTING SNOWMEN

You will need 5 dice, and a pencil and paper.

Take it in turns to throw all five dice. Keep a score of your total – but don't count any 1s or 6s you throw. What's more, for every 1 or 6 you throw, you lose one of your dice. For example, if you threw 2, 1, 4, 6 and 3, you would score 2 + 4 + 3 = 9, and you would only be able to throw three dice next time. Once you have lost all

five dice, you 'melt' and have to drop out of the game. The winner is the one with the highest score.

'S' IS FOR SANTA

You will need to cut 100 small squares from card. Write letters on the cards:
6 each for A, E, I, O, U;
1 each for Q, V, X, Z;
3 each for all the others. Draw a Santa on the rest – these can stand for any letter.

Turn all the squares over with the letters facing down. Take 6 letters each, and take turns to make a word. Replace the letters from the main pile. If you can't make a word, use your turn to take an extra letter. Keep going until all the letters have been used.

The winner is the one with the most letters made into words. Christmas words score double!